Learning Russian

Dear Lynn,

DIANA
FITZGERALD
BRYDEN

*Thank you for your kindness
to me over the past few years,
and for your own beautiful
words.*
love
Diana

LEARNING RUSSIAN

The **Mansfield** Press

Canadian Cataloguing in Publication Data

Bryden, Diana Fitzgerald
    Learning Russian

Poems

ISBN 1-894469-00-3

1. Title

PS8553.R92L42 2000   C811'.54   C00-930570-X

The author would like to acknowledge the generous support of the Canada Council, the Ontario Arts Council and the Toronto Arts Council.

"Inside Toledo" first appeared in *Beds and Shotguns* published by Insomniac Press. "The History of Trains" appeared in *Vintage 96*, a League of Canadian Poets anthology, published by Quarry Press.

Cover design by Bryan Gee
Text design in FF Scala by Colin Christie
Author photo page 64 by Sonia Bibershtein

The **Mansfield** Press
25 MANSFIELD AVENUE, TORONTO, ONTARIO, CANADA. M6J 2A9
Publisher: *Denis De Klerck*

To Susan Olding

Learning Russian

LEARNING RUSSIAN

for Greta Matevossian

The gates are wrought-iron,
tight-hinged and elegant.
I know them at once –
their letters, unscrolling, were meant
for me. Unlock the Cyrillic,
unfasten the gates.
Be patient, wait – not too fast.
They click open, at last...
and here's the garden.

This is like dancing, or poetry.
First the steps, the alphabet,
bring confidence, then clumsiness
as words settle, body submits
to the logic of choreography.
First I must be a child again:
spoonfed my vocabulary.
I get impatient, grab the cutlery,
loot the dark blue dictionary.

How does my child's version of Russia –
exiled poets, snow-covered plains –
elide with London's grey rain
or the harshness of a Welsh valley
whose hills, wet slate,
rush to the bottom, culminate
in a rock bored through by the arrow
that killed a wife's young lover?

I come from an army of dissemblers
hidden – like soldiers, deceptively neat –
between words in a dictionary
now fleshed out: winter,
grandmother, garden. Each word
buzzing with lush sound,
full of the balm of trees and water.

My slippery family long since shed
language, strangeness, Jewishness

as if there were no tomorrow,
no yesterday. As if we could
spring whole and grown from our own foreheads,
awkward, self-made, denying loss.

I promised not to romanticize
but it's not true – I lied.
I'll try not to fall for the ideal past,
but it's warmer than this winter,
more substantial than this backdrop,
easier to hold on to than the train
that pulls away in my dreams at night.

Children scour the past for clues
and mysteries, as if history
were treasure instead of just the past.
Parents and grandparents are confused
by this cosying up to time lost.
Prosaic, unsentimental,
they watch as their children kneel
elbow-deep in books and photos,
brimming with insult, outraged:
"Why didn't you keep the rest
for me? How can you not remember?"

This is the immigrant song, I guess,
the castaway's lament – unfinished,
never arriving, unable to go back
to the home that never was.
But why look for one place?
Why not be content living in between,
where there's more light, more space,
more air? *Half-home* is where I live –
where everything and everyone I love resides.
There's no cradle, no lap
that will truly soothe – and besides,
I want to live ambivalent, unhealed.
I just want to get deep enough
to find out what's there, underneath –
what, if anything, to keep.

But listen: I'm not learning Russian for this –
not some doe-eyed, back-to-my-roots retreat.

For one thing it's too difficult!
And too independent: the language itself defeats
romantic longing – well, not quite –
full of irony and jokes,
it's still steeped in romance.
Here in my throat
its swift water rushes,
between tongue and teeth
sounds of sleep hush
and comfort: rustling trees.

The first time Greta, my friend and teacher,
read Tsvetaeva out loud
in Russian, I cried.
It was as if all longing,
all music, hidden underneath
burst out, made the words vibrate –
past and present collide.

Home

VANYA AT HOME

for Pier Bryden

Having seen *Uncle Vanya* as a child,
I turned away from Chekhov for a while.
In my young womanhood he was too bleak,
his people squanderers, weakened
by degrees of loss
I couldn't yet afford to see.
In those days, I was a character
(Eustacia, Bathsheba or Anna)
in any book I read. Hardy's neurotics, Tolstoy's doomed adulteress
were more enticing than Vanya and his niece;
than country doctors and pompous poets
whose lives were frightening in their quietness.
I was appalled then by confinement –
any constraint that couldn't be overcome
by luck or battle. (I thought all nuns
were god's prisoners, and should be freed by violence!)

When I watched Louis Malle's screen adaptation
of *Uncle Vanya*, I had a revelation.
From the first scene
I was unable to sit back.
I leaned forward, breathless,
anxious and exquisitely awake.
Pain, its source unnameable, was stirred
in me by the actions of these vain,
thin-skinned people, about their business,
surviving boredom and betrayal.
I thought: I'm with family, trapped here,
everyone familiar as an old chair
and as tiresome. A kind of ache accumulates –
of pointless, chafing love
for people I'm embarrassed to be one of:
lazy, articulate, too passive to turn fate –
hypochondriacs whose spiritual torment
"presents as gout," a doctor (Chekhov
or my sister Pier) might say.

Yet so much movement! So much action!
Though throughout the characters do nothing

but talk and worry (about aging, lovelessness, pollution),
and make their small, continuous, awkward motions
to and from each other.
All the drama of disillusionment is there –
the final understanding, by the "good"
that their faithfulness won't be rewarded
and that they are not good, anyway,
just unlucky: thwarted.
Lacking opportunities for sin.

No member of this family
is freer than another, less boxed-in
by domestic obligations. In desperation, Vanya,
small and fat, cruel and funny, taunts Elena –
sensitive pig to her stubborn fox – putting in time
as Sonia tells him, so that the next life might redeem
what was missed in this one.
What a strange concept!
Add time onto time itself, let life escape
so that death will reward you later,
while under feigned resignation: panic.

Everyone heard about the tornado –
its bent thumbs popping the roofs of homes,
farms flattened like paper models
(collapsed as if instructions went wrong).
Precious animals snatched from their places,
torn from the hands of those who lost all in the chase.
And one man's lament, old country music:
"You work all your life and in fifteen seconds it's gone."

Picture a small girl – five, maybe six years old –
sitting in bed at night, awake – are you there yet?
Night-time worrier, she's already adept
at existential anxiety – patrolling the hours
when things go missing: transformed
from door-frames and sweaters to monsters.

Tigers and wolves, watching the crosswalks
wait till she tries to pass: then they'll attack.
Once they have her, they'll keep her forever,
asleep, in helpless suspension.
This is why she sits up in bed with the light on,
haunted by bedtime stories
which, like her clothes and their shadows
turn her house upside down.

I have two fathers, one dead.
He was a butcher, a baker, a poet –
no, he was a pilot
and he had a wooden leg
from the war.

I used to climb inside his leg.
It had a little wooden door,
and when he walked
I bounced inside, a baby plum,
soft and slightly bruised.

He'd take me with him to the park
and lift me out to play,
and when it rained he'd put me back
and carry me all the way home.

It ended on the day he asked
if I would marry his brother.
When I said no he pulled away.
He left without me
and I was locked out of the cool wood forever.

My other father lets me wander
through the gardens he grew up in:
Port of Spain and Elizabethan England.
I swim the flooded gardens of his childhood.
Oranges the size of footballs
fallen from his favourite tree
are glowing in the dark water,
solid suns tipped from the sky.
He tells me: *thou art more lovely
than a summer's day.*

I see him as a young boy,
a fat little scholar
correcting his teacher,
who's just said:
"Emily Dickinson lived on the moors
with her brother and sisters."

"But sir..." Smack!
The teacher clips my father on the head
and trips him out the door,
faster than you can say
Emily Brontë.

My father knows his Emilys.
He spent two years in their company
when the ship from England
bringing his textbooks
sank halfway across the sea.

Boom! The water sucked it down,
swallowed the books, leaving some
floating on the green water,
a sea library,
their wet covers tumbled fruit.

Outside his classroom
my father stands waiting
alone in the hallway,
its walls dappled by orange trees.

My little father sings to me
alone in the dark.
He knows I'm coming.
His small hands are folded while he sings,
and I swim towards him, knowing

he will not shut me out of his garden, no
he won't shut me out of his garden.

If you've read Les Murray's poem
Quintets for Robert Morley
you know something about its author –
and about my father,
who, to his chagrin,
has often been mistaken
for this actor, an error sometimes taken to extremes.

Once a woman so disbelieved
his first shy, then pained disclaimers
that she chased him into the surf
of the Trinidadian beach
where he'd gone home to see his family
and for a hard-earned holiday.

Up to his hips in the foaming waters
of Trinidad, my dad waited
for his pursuer to grow tired,
to stop waving pen and paper,
stop calling with hostile vigour:
"I know it's you, Mr. Morley,
I know it's you!"

The Morley story as we knew it
has fallen out of use.
We've since changed settings,
lost our accents, spread out thin.
And here in Canada, our chosen land,
no one laughs when he's confused
with a celebrated fat man.

As in some nineteenth-century novels,
here a character's outside is taken to reflect
the inner man or woman. If svelte, or beautiful,
then disciplined or virtuous.
Not that this equation's inverse
is more true, but it seems more generous.

I saw Les Murray read once in Toronto.
His poems were intricate and dense,

wild and eloquent, but his listeners
seemed unmoved. Daunted, perhaps
by his accent, Australian,
or by his size, vast.

They were restless, anyway,
waiting for the evening star.
A local writer, beautiful,
who read, head down in shyness
as if ashamed of his own lustre,
or wanting to protect it
from men and women, his admirers
whose leaning, yearning posture
typified the stunned response
to his self-effacing elegance.

During this awkward seduction,
I looked up at the stage where Les
Murray seemed at first
laconic, unperturbed, and then,
purely unconscious as,
exhausted from his flight, he slept.

How long does it take
to get used to a new climate?
To stop grieving for autumn –
slow, heart-piercing season
that, half-unwilling, sheds summer,
puts on its own wet dresses,
sweeps out into the rain,
rustles its way through London's drains
and below, echoes in the sewers.
In autumn water fills the eaves,
pulps the leaves to shadows:
small birds, handprints
on the pavement, wet and brown.

The seasons I knew as a child
were reticent, mild –
distinguished by levels of rain.
Rain, dense and vertical,
made the inner moods
of an uneasy home less brittle –
and softening, less dangerous.
Spring was a breath of dampness,
making light of everything,
opening green skins
and leaving behind a delicate aching.

Here, spring and fall
are shutter-clicks,
a quick split from August –
that long, horrible sulk –
to December, when the sky spits
whiteness, blanching the streets,
and chimney-smoke stiffens,
suddenly upright.
In this cold, I'm either blindly awake,
slapped alert by frigid
rhythms, or stalled,
my thoughts turned rigid.

My family arrived on New Year's Day,
twenty years ago this year.
Since our plane set down
into a blizzard, a white mist
of the unfamiliar, I've stayed
unbelieving in this weather.

I'm addicted to trains.
To their weird homeliness,
which soothes the old ache
of living unmoored
as sitting inside, I imagine the people I pass
to be stitched-down, secured
close to where they were born.

The wheels move in an exile rhythm,
hypnotic, humming.
What's outside seems to beckon
and pull away: the edge of the lake
– smooth, milky water –
a man walking the tracks
head down, as if looking
for his dropped quarter.
The train's cars – boxes of light –
flash past entrances
to desolate places:
hollows, wet fields, pools
where abandoned tools rust. Graves.

Trains lost their innocence
a long time ago,
meeting schedules, moving shipments,
loaded with terrible cargo.
In the books there are maps
whose broken grey lines
show all routes benign –
just parallel tracks.
But the scrape of the wheels
is a rigorous alphabet,
one that won't let us forget.

This old dream, now familiar,
has recurred many times since the first.
Waiting alone on the platform, I'm lost.
Brown floor, high ceilings, cold.
Dream-air cloudy, powdered with dust.
Walls embossed Russian gold.

Now the train leaves the station,
pulling away with a raw exhalation.
My father, whose face I can't see
(or assemble from memory –
he died before my first birthday)
sits inside with a woman. They chat lightly,
turn and look past me.
I start to run, calling. They smile and wave,
– *so long, so long* – eager to leave.

In another dream, another movie,
my father, the hero, leaves Moscow
for the outer reaches of Russia.
The heroine stands on the platform,
smoke curls around her, enhancing her furs.
She rubs flakes of tobacco between her cold fingers.
They fall in slow motion, pepper the snow.

Gold walls, high ceilings.
Powdery light, dust falling.
We swim in light, unmoored, underwater.
A man waves goodbye to his sleeping daughter.
The train's leaving. It's gone.

Toronto

The silence of cities

for Les Murray

I'm in love with the silence of cities –
the breakers we've "built against silence"
as you say, and you're right about this:
cities are never quiet.
But neither are forests or deserts.

My city at night is a forest
or a range of cliffs on the coast.
Trucks make short-cuts, cables hum,
meeting in a wave of sound
that pushes the shore of the dark,
rushing like animals or air.
The morning breaks up into surf:
bird-cries, buses, bells – all start
the acceleration into noise.
The day is a tide, going out.

Perhaps it's a weakness of spirit,
but I cannot live in the country.
Loneliness there drives me mad
and I'm shamed by my own desperation.
The wind in the trees by the water
seems to empty the air from the sky.
I feel myself shrinking, dissolving –
all the borders are falling apart.
I'm awake half the night, resisting
the stifling mound of the dark.

But here, even in winter
when the sky is a transparent lung –
an ungiving page that stays empty –
I'm accompanied, even then
by words that pierce its blankness.
By the pressure, of strangers around me,
that keeps me awake and turned outward.

Across the white yard a neighbour
looks down at the street from his window.
His face is a featureless oval –

a dog waiting at the high fence,
straining to sniff out the distance.
When in summer the air is unbreathing
the same neighbour sleeps in his yard.
I see him at night from my balcony,
then look up in the milky half-light,
as the softening surface splits open –
air is water, trees are shadows,
the rooftops are boat-hulls, floating.

Then the sky is as wide as the outback
and the silence is vibrant and endless.

Untitled

The city is wild.
Half-derelict, it beckons.
A bruised sky opens its arms
and sunken lights tremble,
rocked by damp winds.

The bridge offers up a table of light,
elegiac, monumental.
No cornices, or classical pillars
but a rubbled lot. Train tracks that shake
under a glowing carapace
that cuts into the naked sky.
The ruined, primeval terraces
are sliced apart by rusted wings.

At this time of year, dusk demands witnesses.
All instincts seek light, pulled towards it.
The sky breathes purple. The sun, red no longer,
loses fire with each minute of winter.
Now it runs out in a splash of amber.

In the streets, barely visible to each other,
people are wraiths. Their faces sombre,
sharp with the drawn beauty of winter.
Tossed papers rustle, the lake moves closer;
avenues pulse, new tributaries.
Now a walk to the corner
may lead you to water –
an alley turn into the woods.

LITTLE AUDEN DITTY

At my desk on Tuesday night
I was dreaming, thoughts turned inward
when my eye was caught by a movement of light
in the sky: sunset closing its shirred

red curtain, slit by a narrow trail
of vapour, as if below a failed
flight had ended in disaster.
I thought of Auden's poem about the Old Masters

and that, like the sailors or children
of the poem, I might have sat oblivious –
as they were to the death of Icarus –
while some other would-be angel fell from heaven.

For years, I thought this city was a screen:
that some truer version,
another life – more real,
played over it.

Toronto's so new, illegible.
It's easy to take its cool, reflective face
for a blank, grey wall instead of flesh.
Everyone here is homesick.
The lake's a sink
where all our dreams and origins
might drain away.

Now when I walk through the city's parks and gardens
at night, I feel their movement:
a susurrus, drawn out
through corridors of green.
The concrete breathes.
I hear peacocks in the bushes,
trees that sway with unseen fruit.

There are no peacocks here, of course,
but small, brown birds
who hide in trees, simulating fruit.
Invisible, they make a small bush seem to sing,
and, throbbing in the vines along a wall
add movement to a painted mural.

The statues in our parks
are pint-sized: heroes, turned domestic,
whose purpose is to serve the homesick
with a replica of home: Bolívar, Alexander.
And Jean Sibelius, whose stone eyes saw
a small girl stolen from his garden.

An atheist's prayer

This year has seen the end of the world.
In dreams, processions of refugees unfurl
like snails, dragging the past on their backs.

Here in the city, glazed yellow,
pushed down in its bowl by the stinging heat,
I've been trying to translate my fear.
And to honour the dead,
whose dreams of the end are concrete.

First I went looking for prayers:
two men leave the plague-shocked city
at midnight, for a swim in the harbour.
The sky's milky, the water's warm.
The swimmers step into the sea's amen;
carry their burden, buoyant, between them.
In the grey night they drift, together,
through a passage of literature
so gentle, words become balm.

No gift could be better
than this compassionate diary,
which taught me to stay with what makes me afraid.
Camus felt the suffering of strangers; touching their sores,
he revealed his own soul's tender shores.
His words spread, like music,
– swim away, swim away, pain,
drift to the outer edges –
sombre and restrained.

This summer, a murdered girl's mother slips
into the jewel-blue of her pool.
She carries the burning – lets it float
from her; pain becomes more remote.
It moves out in ripples, into the city,
laps at the heels of reporters and readers,
who find it safer
to focus on one sorrow we've picked a name for
than on the reservoirs, open between us.

Tonight my city's a green bowl,
a cup of green, overflowing
whose light falls translucent, in watery veils.
A chorus is echoing, small and far-off,
and its quiet song reveals
a freshness that forgets nothing:
not death, not even murder.

A MESSAGE FROM JEHOVAH

The summer streets are leafy bowers
where young believers walk in pairs
and trios, a well-matched chorus
of harmony visible on this earth.

Two young women are at my door.
Smiling daughters of Jehovah.
I see no need to be rude, as a rule,
to proselytizers, though I feel

hostility. Why? Their certainty
that they know the way to redemption.
And because the door is always barred
to some kind of heathen – me, for example.

But today my own drawbridge is down, it seems.
One woman asks if I feel alone.
If the bad things that happen leave the impression
that God has abandoned the modern world.

I explain that I don't believe in God.
Because He seems callous? she asks.
No, I answer. We make our own trouble,
abandon each other, and we're alone, now and later.

As I listen to the calm lilt of her voice,
not for the first time and not for the last
I picture the cradle of conviction
swung by a strong, benevolent hand.

But for me, the bough's broken. It was long ago.
Here in the hospital of religion
where belief's a body, faith an intestine,
I have an inoperable blockage.

In a moment of weakness I take a pamphlet.
The pictures are sun-drenched, giddy-hued.
Smiling people, blissed-out and joyous
hold baskets that drip fruit, grain and flowers.

(Salvation never takes place downtown.
In the end, we'll all vacate the cities
and sing through the valleys,
swinging our baskets of fruit, grain and flowers.)

Under the heady illustrations
an anonymous writer discusses the problem
of refugees. Solutions suggested. Repatriation.
I'm disappointed. Unsurprised

and entirely self-contemptuous
at having appeared to begin this romance
when I never intended to travel the distance.
I love the city. I don't want the valley,

and from now on, when I hear the bell
I'll stay in my kitchen. Work at my desk.
Lose a word, break a rhythm, take a half-breath
and continue. They give up soon enough.

Ghosts 2

Early evening:
a sun-struck girl is shouting in the street,
sick with heat and hunger.
She screams at her survival partner,
a man, much older, whose face is rock,
sand-blasted, chipped and pocked.
Last night the man spent all their money.
Tonight, they'll sleep in a ravine.
All day together, she and he
have washed car windows, uninvited.
Fired by sun, glass turns white
– TVs tuned to other channels –
behind which drivers shake their heads,
accelerate, graze the girl's burnt legs
and surf towards fresh lights.

The man turns his face away. Her voice runs down
into a child's uncertain whine –
for money, food and rescue.
They give up at sunset,
work their way north,
carry their bags down into the hollow.
The tides of noise above die out.
Sound turns intimate: whispers, slaps,
and fretful sigh of wind in trees.
Nothing to do in this green furrow
but make a bed
and sleep with birds and ghosts.
Then wake tomorrow, haunted
and still hungry.

Someone's dancing on an old tin floor,
in tap-shoes, pounding out a stiff, erratic rhythm.
No, someone's knocking wildly with a heavy hammer
that echoes every time the blow comes down.

With the noise there's a bitter, sour smell,
lime-green, perforated by ammonia.
A truck, camel-humped with canvas, stands
clamped to the wall of the flat, low building.

The truck looks hot. Steam leaks out
from slits in the canvas. Sheep are bleating.
Dull metal sides gleam in the sun.
The other side there's an open door
and a narrow ramp down which they're thrust,
one by one, towards the hammer blow that knocks out light.
There's a man in the truck, midwifing the sheep,
and for him the noise, the smell and the heat
must be edging close to delirium –
as the sheep still inside smell the blood below
and their dance accelerates: frantic, staccato.

The truck's hidden lip, the sawdust-sticky ramp
are the necessary grit and fuel,
like freight-trains that pass unnoticed at night;
garbage that melts; its soft, rotten smells;
a guilty girl sneaking home at dawn.
All this keeps the oyster seeding.

A jewelled purse glitters on the sidewalk,
dissolving upwards when I pass:
a spray of flies – jet and iridescent. Once I'm gone
they'll go back to what they're feeding on.

GARDEN

In this garden of no Eden, people are sleeping:
a deep, deep, chemical sleep.
Vulnerable plants, heads bent like penitents;
top-heavy flowers trembling on stalks.
Wilted and listing inwards or sideways,
their fingers rustle, subconscious,
remembering the feel of money,
of purses, letters, the touch of a hand.
Fists clench, locked by thumbs
as mouths are locked by cold tongues.
Sometimes it's too heavy, the burden of health.

Restless, the wind moves its hands
over the garden's long green body.
Magnolias have dropped their blossoms
in a silent, overnight explosion.
Sprayed on the grass: crumpled papers,
white pages stained by wine or tea,
surround the feet of the bench-sitters
who ignore them as if they were unread letters.
Sometimes it's too distant, the message of health.

Albert's Blue

A narrow spring wells up from an open-pit mine.
From the top, ragged rings of rock peel down,
unbroken to the bottom lip, which drops
away: water, unearthly lozenge
of radiant blue, so deep the pure
response of spirit and body is fear –
of the savage rock above, that smokes in the heat,
of the long stretch of air swallowed underneath.

Albert paints one blue canvas
all summer, in his grandmother's garage.
Every day he braves the heat
in the tinderbox. Tin walls pulse,
throw out a wave that knocks him flat.
From the cement, he looks up,
tries again to find the source,
then, lost, lies down and falls asleep,
hopes he'll wake inside his painting.
Later, delirious, he staggers out
to the driveway, a disoriented sheep,
wet and trembling in the open light.

With eyes shut, Albert and I both see blue.
At night, it beckons from below.
In memory and dream I descend the mine,
plumb the rock and its darkening vein.
Drop each level, count each ledge
in the dark, depth markings illuminated
by a sudden flare as I pass.

For this colour, you need a compass.
Albert's grandmother scans in vain
for a boat or a star, for navigation.
Is it sea or sky that burns
like this, as only blue can burn?
The throat of the mine, the square on the wall
are remnants of light, the cold heaven
whose eventual pull will take us:
Albert, and me – take us all.

A CHAIR

An empty chair stands on the dock
alone in the blue evening light.
The man who sat there
has gone to get drunk
up at the house with his friends tonight.
Deserted, the chair is a patient ghost
attendant to the horizon:
beyond its square frame
the last drips of sun,
syruped fruit, slip into the river.

Some time later, the man will return,
unaware of the beauty his absence provided.
The sense of his presence suspended
gives the chair – blond wood, legs dented
by restless feet, sun-faded seat-
cover peeling – its grace.

Objects freed from use become numinous:
charged by the lives of their wearers or users.
The scraps of a meal left over.
A dress fanned out on a bed.
A factory vacant at night
watching over the harbour.
All things abandoned.

In the cemetery up the hill
the same names repeat.
Some stones are meant for a couple,
one already under earth.
The other a name beside a blank rectangle.
Smooth, still uncarved, raised up from the marble.

Coke cans are such pretty things.
Wrapped in red and silver wings
of colour, heroic but wistful.
Tears of water shiver
on short pistons.
Smooth concavities sweat at either end.
And the tab, grooved
has been improved:
it won't snap off now when you pull –
one nice CRACK! and then you swill.

ONE WINTER NIGHT

One winter night I travelled
home, the streetcar ride unravelling
in grey and red, a sled
whose glide was staggered
by snow-clogged rails and passengers.

The sky had slowly hollowed,
as light drifted up and blotted out.
The gardens of the hospital
were tucked-in sheets,
the darkened streets a toss
of wires spilled from a box.

In the streetcar, at the back,
a man lit two candles and began to sing.
He was a hospital refugee, in sandals,
bare feet exposed, a medal
pinned to his lapel
and on one hand a plastic ring.

In a melancholy baritone
he sang out streetnames –
"Oz-ing-tone," "Oz-ing-tone" –
brown hand cupped
round yellow-white flame.

A ripple of feeling swept the car,
as we all became part of a formal procession,
transporting grief – that seems to sit
in each of us, always, sifting,
sometimes heart-level, sometimes lower,
down near the soles of our feet.

We coasted in the winter dark,
each street a wave crested by snow.
People fell silent. The singer's dirge
steered our cortege from stop to stop.
Its knife-like comfort a sharp, lonely thrust,
a moment of rare communal grace –
a bite in the crust of isolation.

He stepped off into darkness.
Light flickered in the street
before wind blew it out.

London

Abandonment. Inside the storm.
Light fractures; plates split
apart, gash the sky, spill cloud
and light. The earth
vibrates. No one crosses
the bridge. Green water. Reeds shiver; send ripples
of restlessness. Goosebumps.

The church, a bony finger,
points, warning, to the sky.
Metallic haze. Colour: bronze
and grey. Clouds rushing fields darken
the grass; dipped in shadow like hair in water.
We taste ozone. Throw windows open, feel the chill,
the storm's wet breath.

Far from home, surrounded
by travellers, neither alone
nor with friends. Pulled inside
Toledo, here in London. Waiting
for myself to return.

The British Museum

The sight of all these books has disciplined my nerves.
I'm steeled by their glinting, wrinkled spines.
And now, once I can relax into the curved
shoulders of this room – breathe in its must,
(cool and pure – climate controls subdue the dust) –
I'm freed from my burden: fear of loneliness
in London, now unhomely, city I've lost my grip on.

Early today I phoned the Coroner's Courts,
hoping to get my father's story, finally, straight.
Instead, the thirty-five-year question stays
unsettled permanently. Or is resolved,
its answer given by instinctive truth. "Why
the sudden interest after all this time?"
the clerk asked, kind but sceptical.
I could have said, "Not sudden, just delayed,"
but I forget exactly what I told him.

From the ceiling of this egg-shaped room –
a fragile, shabby Fabergé,
pale blue and milky glass with lead-ribbed crown –
clouds of paint have peeled away.
Someone tapped their spoon
too hard. But here I'm out of the way of harm,
protected by nursery light that's stroked
words from so many; stillness that brings calm
enough to bear the daily weight of living.

All around me, people lean, content
and sober, breathing on their cuddled books.
Pages are held taut – they mustn't be bent
or pressed on by a pen, or smudged.
(The regulations warn, stern and intense
about the vulnerability of paper.)
I want to know what everyone is reading:
business men, Ph.Ds, professors
from the States. My hunger's stirred
by what's in their grocery carts: luxuries
or wholesome foods I'll never buy.
I'm a magpie: everything I see is shiny.

What did the inquest say? He fell
forward: suicide – or slipped back: natural
death. Palms were greased
or simply pressed, feelings spared
and suffering overruled.
I let it go, it's not my story now.
Here inside this egg, the light is clear enough.

Peter's Year

Peter lost a year, but didn't recognize
at first, that it was gone.
It was the year his father died
at work, in an unrecoverable fall,
his grace-giving hands
 – inherited by Peter –
incapable of saving him.

Time split, then reassembled. The children,
Peter and his sister Beth,
went to school, helped their mother –
who seemed most fragile of the three – recover,
began to mark out their careers...

But then, one summer, Peter works
repairing stonework at the church
where his father's buried.
He sees the date on his father's grave and
something breaks.
A discrepancy. The date of death
is a year earlier than he had thought.
What happened to that year?
He asks himself. Where did it go?
What did I do for all that time? Why can't I think?
Questions tighten into knots, his hands seize up
and stop their work. He drops his tools,
watches his fingers whiten and turn stiff.

His tools lie abandoned in the grass. He walks home,
wondering, still looking at his hands.
The year, turned over and over
between his fingers
runs out, and by the time
his mother finds him
Peter has stopped speaking.
Curled into a fœtal mole
on the bedroom floor he stares
inward, as if he can find that year,
dig it out from where it's buried,
and restore what's lost.

The doctor comes, help arrives.
Peter's examined, medicated.
Treatment begins, then finishes.
He comes back home. Moves in again
with his mother. Beth, his younger sister, leaves
for Canada and then, the States.

Time's so light, so hard to hold,
not stone, it's water. Not rock, but sand.
No one asks if Peter found his year
out there in the dark. He doesn't talk
about it, ever, now. He still works
at restoration and,
in one old house, he runs his hand,
for comfort, over walls that undulate
in linen-fold, a lost art that makes dead wood
flow with warmth and grace.

I can't lose an image
once it's planted in my head.
No surgery can excise
a stranger's stolen misery:
the face that fills a slot
in my memory cabinet.

(How many children
have seen an identical vision
in history class: bodies turned over
by the Allies' bulldozers?
Can suffering pictured
induce compassion?)

I squirm at the face, recalled –
a soldier disgraced: convicted spy
for his country's ally,
on his way to prison.
Crying like a stricken child,
dark head against grainy sky,
tarmac, empty airstrip.
An indolent hand
rests on his shoulder –
not comfort but power.
The guard steers him on
as a father might his disappointing son
towards impending discipline.

The prison suit is quilted, white –
a baby's diaper.
The soldier sobs in his swaddling suit,
and it's this image, this theft of his spirit,
that I squeeze my eyes against.
Even as I remember this
he will have stopped crying,
begun living and dying in his new life,
his image overtaken.

Fear of night has forced me to become
a connoisseur of dawn.
I can sniff it, smell it: the gradual shift,
as birds comb the dark, clarify it, sift
all the dust and stars out. Black resolves
into blue, the bruise of night dissolves –
gives itself up for day.

I'm an expert on the music of birds,
I have to be. Their signals mean
that my relief is on its way.
When I can begin to see the sky turn bluish grey,
and the birds are not one or two, but a full chorus,
I can switch off the light
and close my eyes. The pillow turns white
in this grey-blue hour.
The sky softens, pulling down colour.

Every night my fragile boat pushes off,
and I stay awake to navigate
my way and back across the lake.
I can't give up. Can't abdicate
my responsibility to resist
this pure unconsciousness
where inner and outer dark mix,
become their most potent.
From here, without vigilance,
I might never come back.

Who would choose this stricken face to look at
every night and every morning?
Certainly no insomniac,
no one like me. (How did I get to be
such an accomplished coward?)

The background of the painting
is a wakeful hallucination.
I can tell the artist's intimate
with sleep-deprived calculations –
How much longer... How much paler
has the sky become? Was it the nightingale... etcetera.
Van Gokh, they call him here, almost
a rhyme with cough, but harsher.

At first he frightened me, coward that I am.
If you look too fast at his wild and hairy face
he becomes the Wolf Man,
ready to jump down and eat you up.
But look longer, he's a co-conspirator.
A passionate sufferer
with mysterious flecked eyes.
The ridged light behind his head
could be the switch from night to day.
Or the other way. One he dreads,
like me, and the other he longs for.
(Which one, I couldn't say).

He's scratched thick paint
so the undercoat shows through,
specks of red and blue –
as the sky sometimes looks:
an old screen with holes pecked in it.
But what seems the sky
could be a garden, or a tunnel.
It pulls behind him in a spiral –
what he sees waiting,
what keeps him painting.

This is less a portrait
than a shadow in the mirror.
A state of soul, not just a face.
He's laid out his inner self
in the way he's spread and scraped his paints:
discipline, fear and bravery.
Look at his face. One clear eye,
the other smeared and half obscured,
irregular. Now I see
he's alone and sorrowful. Acutely
aware of his own afflictions,
determined to paint them.

I saw his sunflowers yesterday,
and a field he'd painted, gold
for heat and blue for air.
All my favourites – Van Gogh,
El Greco, Pissarro – are masters of light.
And of the contrasts between light and dark.
What I love is the glow, the breaking through,
the irregular journey. A station,
the one in my dreams,
blurred by the bodies of people moving and waiting.
Light coming down, smoke rising up,
a thread of light
that moors me to day
and steers me through night.

Night 3: The Lake

When it comes to night
my instincts are all animal.
Threat. Concealment. Predators.
Breath and heartbeat ratchet up.
When I sleep, I sleep shallow,
spring awake at an echo or touch.

Once I woke into a feral crouch
far on one side of your bed.
Heels quivering, wrists flexed,
open eyes blind –
you had leaned in to touch my neck,
to stop me from grinding my teeth
in some animal dream
and you grazed my ankle
with one of your feet.

I am on the edge of a lake:
icy green-black,
pin-toothed fish, flashes of white,
shining jelly, stars.
Sound is pushed through the trees. Wing-beats.
So slowly, your careful voice
draws me back to a warm room.
Under the flat of your hand
I'm a shivering cat
as you smooth my muscles,
print your breath
on my neck, slowing my pulse
to a metronomical steadiness.

Autograph Birds

At first I didn't realize who they were:
two grey-haired men in speckled jackets,
pacing the ground outside the gates
beside the stage door at the back
of the National Theatre on South Bank.

I passed them on my way to get a ticket.
It was the middle of the day and, finally, warm.
The air was dense and shadowy
still with its unshed weight of water.

The men stepped up and down, rustling,
raising and dropping bird-like heads.
Then I saw their arms tighten, necks spring up,
as a woman with light brown feathers

of hair, jeans and old blue sweater
brushed by them. They flew to her,
swift in recognition of the leader
of their flock. Startled, she fluttered,

pulled away, then began to reemerge,
now calm in camouflage, she settled
herself, dipped her head, held out her arm
and pecked her name in their black books.

NOSTALGIA

When I'm in Toronto, I think of London.
Now I'm in London, I'm thinking of...New York,
of all places. Where I have one uncle, no ties,
and have been perhaps twice.
It's happened.
I've officially become
a professional nostalgic.

Poetry

OLD DOGS

My favourite poets, I'll admit
are despots, tyrants, anti-feminist
old dogs. They've scratched at trees,
pissed on bark and legs for years.
When strangers approach
they snarl and flatten wrinkled ears.
But need is subversive. I dig my way
through tunnels while they drowse –
steal what I want from under them
and leave before they catch my scent.

Sour and cynical, dry with ennui,
these old-fashioned singers of beautiful songs
show their true colours in the dark.
I've gone swimming at night
with one fat poet, who lies on his back –
a huge mammal, singing to me.
He calls from the water,
bursts up, his diver's wet head
fizzing out of the sea.
A supple boy laughs
at the old monster, wriggles
out of his crusted skin.
If in daylight I gnash my teeth
at his windy proclamations,
now he, or one of the others
spouts plumes of midnight water,
tossing up jewels, eggs, crisp white onions
clean and full of electric juice.

I choose my muses, unwelcomed by them –
who cares if they want me, dogmatic old men!

LETTER TO JOSEPH

after Marina Tsvetaeva

Today, of course, it's cold – tell me,
Joseph, is this too bold?
Saying your name like this?
After the first shyness – what?
I'm suddenly hot, ashamed
of my unearned grief.

We never drank anything together,
no letters were sent between us,
but I miss you, dear interpreter.
No one else quite fits your niche,
sits on your step, or
has your peppery mixture
of irony, impatience and belief.

Friend in need, friend in words,
you've given me heartburn
more than once. I've tried to eat
your poems and essays whole, at a sitting.
Professor, unconscious father, scold,
old-before-old-age mister, listen:
if you can still be heard, you're not gone –
that's my conclusion.

And I still hear your night-time voice,
still see your light on,
still enjoy the jokes you play
with collapsible time:
twentieth century, Marchember.
(You refuse to be symbolic, but remember
all the arbitrary weight of history's choice).

This is presumptuous, I know,
and childish – a vain attempt
to reach you, but I send this letter
anyway, for your collection.
There are people at your funeral,
friends at your memorial,
monuments who, being famous,

play themselves – stand in
for those of us who watch
as the snow's whipped off the roof-tops
by irascible winds.

Wind-chill today is minus twenty,
smoke scatters wildly,
freed from its frigid, upright stream,
from seeming semi-solid.
I'm in my kitchen,
all transmitters tuned to you.
Joseph, Joe, Mr. B.,
I send you this letter,
like the one M. sent to R.,
her *New Year Letter*, unpeeled by you,
so deftly, skin-by-skin.

At least when she wrote to him
she could claim to be familiar –
to have shared an earthly correspondence.
When I hear news
of the end of your life
from a disembodied, unknown voice,
I have no excuse.
I can't say "I knew him," so I'll lie,
say something else: the puppy died,
my lover left, it's that time again....

Surely, Joseph, this is friendship.
There's no need for any contact
other than your lips
forming words, your pen-scratch
on paper, your *spoken part*.
For you, now, there's no more noise.
No sleeve-tuggers keep you
from your inner voice –
of course, no loved ones, either.
But we who miss you –
readers, family, friends – will still send news.

By the lake

for Marina Tsvetaeva

I'll sing for you by water, in the middle of winter
– the past stretched tight as a wire between us.
By the lake, the city turns into Russia.
The ice shelves are steppes, sloping down to its edge,
the geese arch their necks; unscroll into script.
The hem of my skirt is a snow-salted lip.
My eyes are small throats, open with longing
– an ice thirst, white and blue,
like the summer houses at Tarusa.
The water below is thick as black tea,
and *you are my sugar. I need you like sugar.*

There are holes in life where the dead fit.
Slipping their hands into my pockets,
their touch is like air, soft and expected.
At this moment, the seam is apparent
as time stretches out between past and present.
The ice at my feet crackles with messages.
The lake underneath is counting its losses.
Your words are a whisper that comes from the lake.
What you say is a secret, held lightly between us –
one I'm straining to hear as the ice starts to break.

Two poets. One a field.
The other a wave on a white-hot beach.
One coastal, the other inland,
both beginning in the dark.
One stays earth-bound, turning stones;
digs a space for silence.
The other makes words do the work of weather:
fill sails, shed green, burn.
Does each man sit up at night,
I wonder, and read the other?
Then ask himself: how did he find
that cool breath, there?
How did he start that flame?

I've often been ashamed of the vagueness of my past.
No sturdy set of ancestors, no climate,
or place, firm enough in memory
to signify as history.
And in my house of unconnecting rooms
there's no floor-plan. Bedrooms, kitchens, tombs,
are all sealed off from one another.
We're ghosts, our families so shadowy
we barely make up one.
Runners, rope-cutters, floaters:
lost islands in grey seas.

My father and his home were glass,
invisible but dangerous. The lines, dark blue
painted on his windows
were meant to stop birds flying through.
My second father is the son
of a colonial export-import man.
His ancestors were Scottish, old
sheepfarmers and stealers. They sold
their goods, drifted out
to Trinidad, England, Canada.
Others, Jews, came to Jamaica
from Curaçao. (Dad's mother, irascible,
stubborn, married his father, a younger man
who then chased younger women...all that's predictable.)

I think of my parents as out of step
with each other, half asleep;
awkward in new skins and clothes.
Struggling with language
that each should be adept at.
Their lives have been dislodged,
they've crossed seas so many times,
finally away from each other,
without understanding the point of the journey,
if it had any.

I'm floating or flying too, I see that.
But towards who, or what

I don't know yet.
When I was younger I wanted things plainer –
less muddled, more noble.
Not a bunch of rootless opportunists,
spies, reluctant Jews, suicides whose exits,
to avoid hurt feelings, were called accidents.

What I thought, as a girl, and I believe
my second father taught me this,
is that there's nothing tangible
between us, no inheritance
but words – his,
and later, mine.
If words and their beauty
are untrustworthy,
I've learned to respect them
as much as any other tool.
They've made their imprint on my father
as another man's implements
would mark his hands.

And the disconnectedness I used to think was lack
now I know is luck. Poetry is symmetry.

DIANA FITZGERALD BRYDEN
lives and writes in Toronto.